D1560333

SICILY Photography by Rosario Bonavoglia Text by Donatella Trotta Published by Universe

SICILY

BY ROSARIO BONAVOGLIA

INTRODUCTION *by* *DONATELLA TROTTA*

UNIVERSE

PHOTOGRAPHY: Rosario Bonavoglia
TEXT: Donatella Trotta
TRANSLATION: Philip Rogosky
EDITOR: Elizabeth Smith
PHOTOGRAPHIC ADVISOR AND EDITOR: Jules Labat
PHOTOGRAPH AND TEXT COORDINATION: Rosario Bonavoglia, Francesca Ventura

FIRST PUBLISHED IN THE UNITES STATES OF AMERICA IN 2000 BY:
Universe Publishing
A Division of Rizzoli International Publications, Inc.
300 Park Ave South
New York, NY 10010

2000 2001 2002 2003 2004 2005
10 9 8 7 6 5 4 3 2 1

Printed in Italy

DESIGN: Opto

"AS CHAGALL, I WOULD CAPTURE THIS LAND
IN THE STILL OX'S EYE.
RATHER THAN A SLOW CAROUSEL OF IMAGES,
A NOSTALGIC HALO: NOTHING BUT
THIS CURDLED CLOUDS,
THE SLOW DESCENT OF CROWS;
THE CHARRED STUBBLE, THE SPARSE TREES,
A FILIGREE IMPRESSION"

Leonardo Sciascia

INTRODUCTION

Isole
Eolie o Lipari
Stromboli Isl.
Salina Isl.
Lipari Isl.
Vulcano Isl.
Tindari
Messina
Cefalu
S. Stefano di Camastra
Palermo
Sperlinga
Geraci Siculo
Petralia
Gangi
San Vito lo Capo
Monreale
Segesta
Egadi Isl.
Bonagia
Erice
Trapani
Ciminna
Favignanza
Levanzo
Prizzi
EAST SICILY
Etna
Cammarata
Mozia Isl.
Marsala
SICILY
Acireale
Acitrezza
Catania
Mazara del Vallo
Enna
WESTERN SICILY
Caltanissetta
Piazza Armerina
Agrigento
Siracusa
Caltagirone
Noto
SOUTHERN SICILY
Vindicari
Marzameni
Ragusa
Modica
Scicli
Pachino

SICILY? "IT IS LIKE ONE GREAT BOOK. Full of signs, wounds, and scars. A book I reread continuously, identifying and deciphering new aspects and meanings to it." Sicily is, if not the direct mirror, a precise metaphor of Italy. In the summer of 1997, I met the eminent Sicilian writer Vincenzo Consolo provided me with this outline of his own perspective on the island, an island whose natives are at once its sons and stepsons, destined to a relationship that is alternatingly intimate and distant. Consolo's concept seems a fitting viaticum to the approach that Rosario Bonavoglia has taken in his photographic voyage throughout the "great book" that is Sicily, "reading" – and recounting iconographically – its myriad signs. These accomplished and often startling images are replete with multiple layers of significance, and are distinguished by a vibrant chromatic register full of energy and spontaneity. It is the same canon applied by the author in his two previous publications on New York and on the Divine Amalfi Coast. The approach reflects the peculiar sensitivity of a *deracine* coupled with a mature photographic style inspired to the lesson of National Geographic aesthetics and documentation.

This book is a voyage to the very heart of Sicily – a land of paradox and excess, of contrast and contaminations, a land where awe-inspiring nature meets with a cultural heritage dating back more than a thousand years. We are led by the informed eye of a street photographer who is acutely aware, as Antonio Machado put it, that "there is no way, the way is going." Together with Bonavoglia we take a sort of Grand Tour that, apart from its physical, geographical, conceptual, and photographic significance is, above all, spiritual. A trip to the heart of this polymorphic, kaleidoscopic "continent," almost a separate (multicentered, pluralistic, and often hyperbolic) nation – it is by no coincidence that Goethe remarks in his Italian Voyage: "Had I not seen Sicily, my impression of Italy would have remained imperfect" (Palermo, April 13 1787).

In an often reiterated opinion, voiced by both local and foreign writers, Sicily has been considered the perfect place for an "ideal voyage," for its profound cultural backdrop and for the extreme variety of scenery in such a relatively limited expanse. Indeed, for some, traveling through Sicily – an island of shadows and light, burgeoning with vitality and death, a melting pot of races and a crossroads of cultures – is an adventure unlike any other. It is an undertaking of risk, of anxiety: if travelling is as creative an enterprise as the seduction of one's beloved, the painting of a masterpiece, or the composition of an unforgettable melody, then to travel in Sicily is a challenge beyond comparison. It is the challenge.

Bonavoglia accepts this challenge, armed only with his camera. Sicily's challenge was accepted and won by way of the photographer's worldly yet spiritual, anthropologically inquisitive pilgrimage in search of a "Sicilian nature," transfigured as icons that capture the inevitable oscillation between the immediacy of the present and the depth of the past. In contrast to those who might imagine the region as a land of exotic remembrances, to others, such as Bonavoglia, Sicily is a place where the roots of life itself are apparent. In this sense, the voyage through Sicily is, first and foremost, a voyage through oneself. It is a voyage requiring full appreciation of the scenery Sicily has to offer. Scenes and portraits – one would almost want to call them paintings, impressionist or expressionist, surrealist or naturalist – have been brought to photographic paper through a lens that is guided by the author's Ulysses-like peregrination. The island's sites, landscapes and monuments, popular festivals, its artisans and their timeless faces, are all constituent elements of a side of Sicily that is often misread, despite its widespread notoriety.

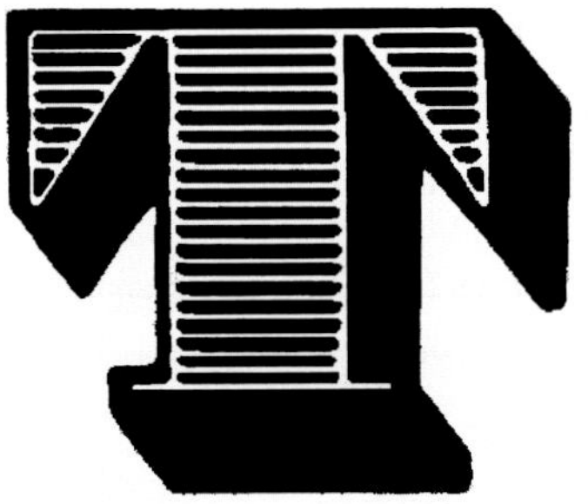

hese details of the great fresco of Sicilian heritage are woven into the fabric of a magnificent and theatrical open-air museum, a treasure trove of the riches of a collective memory, threaded through with light and darkness, with the bitter and sweet of its eruptions of vitality and flashes of death. It is precisely these overwhelming, dialectic forces – irrevocably fixed in this book in unique moments of chromatic intensity – that are the leitmotif of Bonavoglia's Sicilian photographs. As in his previous works on New York and the coast of Amalfi, he has again demonstrated his ability to approach a new territory and its population – and this time the contact is with an "islander mood" that defies decipherment – "with other eyes," in Marcel Proust's words. They are the estranged (but not extraneous) eyes of the non-native; it is from this perspective that he is able to capture heretofore unnoticed aspects of situations wasted by cliché and by their progressive oblivion. He participates in those situations vibrantly and with wonder, as would a child, and thus transmits a very intimate sensation of marvel and emotion, directly to the viewer of his photographs, in accord with André Gide's idea that the importance is in your gaze, and not in the object observed.

Studded as it is with capturing sensory provocations, Bonavoglia's photographs are the stunning evidence of a quest undertaken in search of the manifest, authentic, and vital side of Sicily, more so than of its imaginary, literary, and legendary side. This is a Sicily composed of numerous Sicilies, revisited on every page through the boldly manifest colors of its seas and skies, its sun-struck hills and countrysides, the most secluded and concealed nooks of its harsh mountains, through the myriad villages clinging in clusters to their mountainsides along the sparse enclave the 1,039 km coastline affords, without forgetting its major cities, millennial cradles to the history of more than one civilization. and along the sparse coastline. Sicily is a key to the history of more than one civilization.

"THE LAND OF SICILY IS A COFFER TO WHICH THERE IS NO KEY."

Father Primo Mazzolari

he history of the island of Sicily, as reflected in the photographs that make up this book, is a never-ending balancing act between the certainties of tradition and the uncertainty of existence. From its early origins in the late Paleolithic era (8000 to 7000 B.C.) through the Greek and Roman centuries, during the Arab, Norman-Svevian, and Spanish periods, and up to the modern day, the symbolic bridge that Sicily represents – connecting Europe and Africa, and East and West – has acquired a spiritual importance. The momentous impact of the religious, cultural, and ethnic stratifications, fusions, and cross-breedings that this Mediterranean crossroads has witnessed is condensed and even sublimated in the various legs of the author's epistemic trip. He has crossed the island every which way and during all seasons – since Sicily is to be visited year round – exercising both respect and stamina, and discretion and curiosity as a participating observer. Thus he is welcomed by the local populace as one of their own. The hospitality he experienced is evident in many photographs (for instance, in those of the *mattanza* rites in Favignana). This welcome might be conceived as an "inner voice" (or "gaze," indeed) – part of the warm embrace of an archaic Mediterranean *mater matuta* of the plethora of archeological finds spread throughout the museums of southern Italy. Before it became Sicily (named after the Siculi people, who inhabited the island together with the Sicani and the Elimi), the region was known as Trinacria, the isle of three capes, "Capo Peloro," "Capo Passero," and "Capo Lilibeo," with its crown of minor islands (the Eolian islands, Ustica, the Egadi islands, Pantelleria, and the Pelagic islands), overlooking three seas (the Tyrrhenian, the Ionic, and the Mediterranean). The island was finally split into three parts by the Moors: the Mazara valley to the west, the Noto valley to the southeast, and the Demone valley to the northeast.

Its trilateral shape may stand as a symbol of its exceptional intrinsic transcendence (the eye of God has the same shape in Catholic imagery); traditionally its isosceles triangle has been the basis of a figure composed of three feminine legs connected to a central female head, as a representation of Trinacria. Frequently, this island-woman figure of classical iconography is adorned with ears of wheat, barley, and other grains, in a clear reference to the legend of Ceres, or Kore, the mythical maiden who is, perhaps, the originator of the entire galaxy of mythologies.

It is hardly by chance, therefore, that this book opens with a picture of rural pastorage (with a vaguely Anatolian flavor), and takes its initial steps in the area of Enna, the least well known, the least exploited "stony core" of the big island. Sicily was the first Italian region with an autonomous statute (as of May 15, 1946); it is the largest of all the twenty regions of Italy and the third most densely populated (counting more than 5 million inhabitants, a full 9 percent of the national total). Its soil is rich in fire, poor in water and, and absolutely sun-drenched: the island averages two thousand hours of light per year – Catania, in eastern Sicily and Europe's sunniest city, averages 2,518 hours per year. Beyond the obvious allegorical fascination of many a historical traveler, Sicily thus offers its riches also to those seeking to profit from its environmental magnetism, or those who wish to base their heliotherapy there.

Nearly two-thirds of Sicily consists of hillsides, a quarter is mountainous, and a mere 14 percent of its expanse is composed of valleys and plains. The relative figures for the whole of Italy are 42, 35, and 23 percent. Such figures are eloquent: the prevalence of 86 percent hills and mountains explain the earth-bound and shepherding traditions in its settlements, while also belying the commonplace traditions of a principally maritime Sicily. Nor is it a land of mere juxtaposition: the true soul of Sicily is manifold, the result of the syncretism of at least two worlds, identified as early as the eleventh century by Edrisi, the Arab court geographer to King Ruggero the Norman: to one side are the Islamic influences stemming from the southeastern Mediterranean area; to the other is the Western culture of the European Middle Ages. The former is a window open to the Greek culture influences of the Orient, the latter a filter permeable to the tendencies of occidental Carthage. In the population, and even in literature, this age-old spiritual dualism has resulted in the alternation of an existential skepticism with a lucid, sharp rationalism, giving rise to a potent penchant for visionary, onirical, imaginative thought.

The contrasting Eastern and Western faces of Sicily find an equivalent expression in its literature. On the one side is the mythical, lyrical, evocative, and metaphysical school, in which form is paramount (two authors who come to mind are Salvatore Quasimodo and Lucio Piccolo); on the other is the historicist, dialectic, logical, civilist school, balanced between the sophistry and illusionism of Pirandello, the realism of Verga, the harangues of Sciascia, and the engagement of Vittorini, without mentioning Borgese, Brancati, and Lampedusa. Divided as it is between European rationale and African magic, Sicily's overabundance of identity make it, as the sociologist Antonino Buttitta once put it, "the ideal testing ground for any explanatory model of the human condition and of the history of mankind – only not of itself." In other words, a coffer without a key.

It is precisely this coffer, this stronghold of *preziosi* and surprises, that Bonavoglia has attempted to disclose, discreetly wielding the passe-partout of a concrete existential perspective, a view from within a lived experience, rather than the crowbar of abstract, grid-like categories of interpretation. His work combines that of a traveler (and not of a tourist: he first learned to travel, and only then traveled to learn) and that of a photographer for whom the words of Cartier-Bresson ring especially true: photography is "holding your breath, while all your faculties converge on fixing the fleeting moment; only then does the captured image represent an immense physical and intellectual satisfaction." Because "to photograph is to recognize, in the space of a single instant, a fraction of a second, the occurrence of an event. To put one's mind, eye, and heart all on the same line of focus. It is a way of life."

"ALL THE ISLAND IS A MEDDLE OF MOURNING AND LIGHT."

Gesualdo Bufalino

Given the approach described, the photographs on the following pages are messengers of emotions, rather than of rationalization, social comment, or critique of Sicily. They are fragments of an enamored wandering in a land of seduction. In Bonavoglia's particular style, the images are orchestrated according to their colors: the yellow of *trazzere*, of dunes and sulphur; the gold of stone, of sunsets, wheatfields, and wine harvests; the green of its gardens, its rolling hillsides fading into brown, or into the gray of its urban outskirts; the pink of local stone, farmyards, and flower-showers; the white of the salt lakes, and of the houses on the Eolian islands; the iridescent glow of the ceramic artistry; and more still: the red and black of the volcanoes, of local festivals, of neighborhood markets. An entire spectrum of colors unfolds before us (entirely without the use of filters), often the result of the pathos and tension that runs between mankind and the realm of the sacred – a particularly strong force in Sicily; other times reflecting the intense interrelationship beween man and animal.

It would seem, fundamentally, that the gamut of emotions deployed derives from the spontaneous anthropological inclination of the author, whereby he searches for the essence of the Sicilian soul – often diluted in the routines of daily life – at the heart of processions and ritual recurrences, in religious celebrations and mysterical representations that survive to this day, handed down with obstination from generation to generation, even in the simplest (and youngest) social circles in Sicily. We attempt to link past and present is that of a people profoundly attached to their ethnic identity and homeland in the face of the century-old menace of extinction. On this ground, the author avoids painting a glossier picture than life; and along this line he strings together snapshots, photographs, and sequences that transcend the déjà-vu, coalescing sensations, details, and even ironies in a form similar to the evocative synthesis of the *haiku*, the Japanese poem that, in the space of a mere three phrases (of 5, 7, 5 syllables) alludes, through its lyrical microcosm, to a macrocosm conditioned by the full immersion into nature as far as it governs culture.

The author has chosen to begin his journey in the southwestern region of Sicily (purposely excepting the radiant isles of Pantelleria, Linosa, and Lampedusa), with its nearly African sea, a rugged, wild mountainous interior, a harsh, rough, "world apart," peppered with the remains of ancient civilizations whose origins lie with the Mediterranean seafarers who found hospitality in Agrigento, Eraclea, and Sciacca. It is in the barren countryside near ENNA, chosen as the eloquent opening image, and in the silently hostile surroundings of CAMMARATA, located in the highest mountains of the Sicani chain, that the author initiates his tour of reconnaissance, concentrically circling the island as would an eagle, from the stony inner center toward the outermost realities that Sicily has to offer in a voyage of light.

In Enna, earlier Henna (and then Castrogiovanni), at 931 meters above sea level, the highest of Italy's *capoluoghi* known by the Romans as the Umbilicus Siciliae, the "navel" of Sicily, Bonavoglia has chosen to photograph the Norman CASTELLO DI LOMBARDIA, an impressive fortress against the azure sky, the setting sun gilding the perfect geometry of its six towers (that remain from an original twenty). In ancient times, the area was home to a cult of Ceres, the goddess of harvests and of fertility, the unfortunate mother of Proserpina, the beautiful maiden who drowned while playing along the shore of the lake of Pergusa and who was abducted by Pluto and held hostage in his underworld for six months a year, as her mother was able to obtain the right to the other six months from Zeus.

A little further, in PRIZZI, a fortified, medieval village with Punic-Roman origins, Bonavoglia captures moments of great expressiveness. The *ballu de li diavuli*, the "devil's dance," is an Eastertime ritual in which the men of the town, dressed as horned red devils (and as yellow representatives of Death) engage in energetic dances to a band playing music with an Iberic sound, in a symbolic duel between Good and Evil – between life and its end – that takes place among a sea of onlookers that fill the narrow streets decorated by the peculiar local murales. In the end, it is the pale, crowned Virgin Mary – the black-clad *Mater dolorosa*, dressed to perfection by a loving swarm of furrowed farmer's hands – who wins the battle, as befits this "reverse apocalypse," a spectacular, existential scene, that reveals above all a choral, indeed theatrical, desire of self-affirmation, and of survival.

The voyage continues into the heart of NORTHWEST SICILY, the part of the island most exposed, throughout the centuries, to contact with other civilizations, be it the Phoenicians (who colonized Mozia and founded the harbor towns of Palermo and Solunto), the Greeks, or the Arab Moors, who disembarked in Marsala and went on to conquer the entire island. The choice of destinations is vast in this area, where a variety of splendid natural phenomena (in the countryside around Trapani, near Belice, or on toward the Madonìe) gives way to extended areas environmentally devastated by urban expansion (from Palermo to Castellammare). There are important archaeological sites (among them Segesta, Selinunte, Solunto, Mozia), masterpieces of medieval architecture (Erice, Cefalù, Nicosìa, Sperlinga, and the two Petralìe), and corners of breathtaking coastline around the Egadi islands (including Levanzo and Favignana). Here again Bonavoglia chooses a personal itinerary that begins with the timeless significance of SPERLINGA, seen from a distance, seemingly hewn directly from the mossy rock face on which it is perched (where until recently one could visit the cave dwellings of prehistoric troglodytes), a theater of the ultimate desperate attempt of resistance by the French troops during the Vespri battle. Bonavoglia moves on the vision of GANGI: virtually a cloak of houses draped over the curves of a hill overlooking the Nebrodi and the Madonìe, dominated by the Ventimiglia castle. The members of this ancient family, related to Frederick II of Suevia, king of Sicily, and emperor of the Holy Roman Empire (his daughter Emma married Guglielmo, count of Ventimiglia, and gave birth to Enrico, count of Geraci), were responsible for the renewed cultivation of falcon hunting, an art about which the young Stupor Mundi wrote a weighty tractate between 1236 and 1240 – to this day considered the unsurpassed bible of falconry.

imilarly virile histories inspired the author to visit GERACI SICULO (lying at 1,077 meters above sea level). Here, in the city once known as Iera, or vulture in Greek (and this is one of the former Greek towns farthest inland), home to many religious and folkloric traditions (from the annual Joust of the Ventimiglia, with its accompanying procession in costume, to the Shepherds Cavalcata, a sort of homage paid to the Holy Sacrament), among timeless dark-faced hidalgos participating in the training of hunting falcons, Bonavoglia captures several images that play on the double profiles of predators and humans. The pictures that follow these also deal with animals, as in the charming festive nuptial procession on mule-back, held in PETRALIA SOTTANA. Although this last is a renowned site for tourism in the Madonìe area, the author is not captured so much by the historic monuments as by the animated sequences of the vivid Ballo della Cordella, a picturesque evocation of ancient wedding ceremonies in the crescendo of a collective participation in life.

Then it's time to turn toward the Tyrrhenian coast, to CEFALÙ, the maritime stronghold during the Roman rule of the Mediterranean from the third century B.C. to the second century A.D., as well as during the western affirmation of Byzantium during the ninth century, and during the Sicilian period of Islam, of which Cefalù was a principal center until the year 1064, when the Normans captured the town from its Arab rulers and refounded it as a symbol of the restoration of Christianity in the west of Sicily. What we see here is the marvelous facade of the cathedral founded by Ruggero II (as legend has it, in return for the safe landing he had been granted in Cefalù during a wild storm). Then the gaze turns to SANTO STEFANO DI CAMASTRA (called Santo Stefano di Mistretta until 1812), where the renowned multicolored ceramics steal the show.

The town of MEZZOJUSO (a name derived from "Manzil Jusuf," the village of Joseph, which referred to an Arabic construction that predated this hamlet where Albanian refugees found shelter in the fifteenth century while fleeing the advancing Turks) is represented by a beautiful detail of a horsetail decorated in purple, and by the scenes of the *cunnuta*, a day-long feast celebrated on the day of San Giuseppe, with the white-shirted band resting against the backdrop of the main church of the Annunciation, decked out in Mexican-style lights. (The church, of Norman origin and Latin rites, shares the stage in Mezzojuso with the GREEK-RITE, 16th century church of San Niccolò; both were restored during the Baroque era.)

The photographer's eye is further attracted by a farmer's house in CIMINNA, in a valley south to Anania's peak, portrayed in pastels, as well as by several nighttime scenes of the surreal procession in full costume, depicting the martyrdom of Saint Vito. In the hills on the outskirts of Palermo, a lone, aged horseman is caught as he playfully whips the waterhole where his horse is drinking. Here we are only a stone's throw from the capital, and a detour to Monreale (five miles from Palermo) is a must: we are treated to the motley testimony of its vivid folklore (the detail of a colorful market cart), artisan handicrafts (ceramics, their mirror image broken in several layers of shop-window reflections), and the typical puppets of the Opera dei Pupi.

The city of PALERMO, "Panormos" to the Phoenicians, a flourishing harbor under the Romans, a city of marvels under the Arabs, for whom it rivaled Cordoba and Cairo, and finally capital of the Norman reign, has an initially unsettling effect on Bonavoglia. He seems struck by the decadence of this important metropolis, the signs of the ruinous modern, postwar, and contemporary periods undoing the second splendor Palermo had experienced, and by things architectural, civil, and religious, dating to the seventeenth and eighteenth centuries. It is no coincidence that the Palermo sequence of photographs begins with a macabre picture of the Cappuccini crypt, and ends instead with the joyous festivities in honor of the patron saint, Santa Rosalia, carried on her huge, colorful papier-maché throne. Even in the initial image, an extraordinary triumph of death, the embalmed skeletons of priests and nobility dressed in their most extravagant finery, laid out according to status and profession in otherworldly ostentation, Bonavoglia depicts the crypt in a clement light, the soft aura of blue and virginal white lace surrounding the three mummies, their hands laid in prayer on palm leaves – a symbol of the resurrection – beneath a black crucifix. Moving between the display of death (exposed and thus exorcised) and the promise of life as represented by Santa Rosalia, known as the "patron of the Dead," who saved Palermo from the plague in 1624, the photographer's optimism allows him to capture fragments of life in Palermo, often purposely at night, be it details of significant monuments or of day-to-day life. These are theatrical moments: the curious expression of the groom in full dress, the gathering of children in Piazza Marina, or the grimace of the fishmonger – in the livid, purple light reminiscent of a *mattanza* – beheading a tuna fish at the daily market of Ballarò, the city's southernmost, suk-like market. Here, Palermo show its affinities with Cuba and Cairo: the south of the world, where the parabole of civilization encounters the continuous cycle of decadence and renaissance.

From Palermo on to SEGESTA, a passage into the full flora of the Mediterranean and into the archeological heart of the island is marked by a ghostlike nighttime image of the Greek temple, magnificently isolated on its hill in a wide valley: it is a dreamlike apparition, a perfect synthesis of the light and mourning that are intertwined and woven throughout the pages of this book. They are again symbolized in the almost Arabic profiles of the boy and girl in black period dress, photographed in ERICE against a backdrop of sunstruck houses and the stone structure of the Duomo. The town, a focal point for artistry from its earliest origins (founded by Eris, son of Venus and Butus, who became king of the Elimi, who were based in nearby Segesta), is remarkably intact, and remains a center of exceptional natural and cultural interest (for its history, its architecture, and its riches). This curiously triangular town was host to ancient Punic cults, such as that honoring the goddess of fertility, beauty, and love, Astarte, who was later reinterpreted as Aphrodite by the Greeks and as Venus by the Romans. Seafarers and pilgrims brought offerings of all sorts and copulated with the *hierodule*, the high priestesses who practiced a form of sacred prostitution to honor a local version of the goddess remembered as the Venere Ericina, on the site of the temple whose ancient location has been identified inside the so-called Castle of Venus, erected on its isolated crag between the twelfth and thirteenth centuries.

The multiethnic crossbreeding strikes the eye also in the photographs of MAZARA DEL VALLO, considered the most African of all the Sicilian cities. Bonavoglia presents the city with a learned detail of the bas-relief on the portal of the cathedral (originally founded in 1093 and subsequently rebuilt in 1690–94) showing Count Ruggero the Norman astride his horse, and below him a stricken Muslim. Prior to Norman conquest, since the year 827, Mazara del Vallo had been under Arab rule, and had known a period of glory deemed "exceptional" by the court geographer Edrisi. Nowadays Mazara's importance lies in its fishing industry. It hosts a sizable community of Tunisian workers, employed on the fishing boats, who are perfectly at home in the casbah in the middle of town – in one striking portrait we find nostalgia in the eyes of a fisherman as he looks out of the porthole of his boat.

Tracking north along the coast from Marsala to Trapani, passing the archeological riddle (only recently solved) of MOZIA – the small Punic island in the lagoon named Stagnone, razed in 997 B.C. by Dionisio II of Siracusa – we arrive at the magical windmills looming over their salt lakes in the surreal twilight. Again, northern Europe is juxtaposed with Africa: the current reality of the strenuous job of simply surviving here (seen especially in the image of the worker collecting salt) contrasts with the past, as pictured in the refined Greek marble youth, perhaps a charioteer, of Near Eastern origin, on display at the museum of Mozia, whose patron was an Englishman, John Whitaker.

TRAPANI (which takes its name from a latinization of the original dialect name drepana meaning "sickle," as a reference to the shape of the town stretched around its bay) is portrayed in this book exclusively as a city of sacred mysteries: the images are those of the annual Easter procession held on Good Friday. We are at a pivotal point in the voyage, an anthropological and symbolic-expressive crux. The tireless parade (lasting twenty-two uninterrupted hours), in which twenty statues depicting separate instances of the Passion of Christ (made of wood or of papier-maché and dating back to the sixteenth and seventeenth centuries) are marched through town, accompanied by groups representing all the traditional occupations (the *ceti*: the fishermen, farmers, and artisans) to the sound of the music played by bands and the invocations of the participating parishers, is indeed, as has been observed, a full-fledged "collective psychodrama." It is the tragedy of the passion and death of the Messiah, it is the mystery of his resurrection, of eternal life, played out in the piazza, and acted out in the streets in spontaneous theater similar to the Opera dei Pupi. The first image of the series is indicative: the audience standing behind the barriers appears to be the actors, rather than the spectators, of this large-scale *commedia umana*. Similarly, this effect is evident in the gesture of the dark girl in her red dress, with her offering of wheat, a message of new life to follow the ritualized death, solemnly enacted by the exhausted followers, their expression almost mirroring the suffering depicted in the statues they carry through the streets.

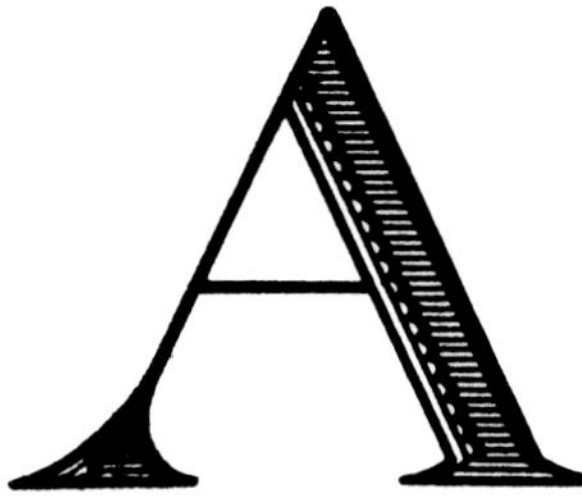

fter the crowds, there follows a moment of quiet: the next stop on the trip is at Trapani's old tuna factory, where in harsh, sun-stricken surroundings, the ancient, totemic black boats of BONAGÌA serve as reminders of a past that has survived to this day. In these photographs, we have a prelude to another central moment of the voyage, the *mattanza* (from the Spanish matar, "to kill"), the massacre of tuna fish as practiced on the island of FAVIGNANA. We approach the scene in steps: first a calm row of fishing boats, then the anticipatory tension captured visually in the gestures of a powerful armwrestle among fishermen, followed by an abstract perspective of the nets in the water, governed by the rais, the head of the hunt, Cataldo. And then, suddenly, the full drama erupts in a spectacle of shooting water and racing fins caught in the carefully prepared, deadly trap, the camera della morte. The apex of the ritual is reached in a crescendo of propitiatory prayers and chanting, even declarations of love addressed to the fish (referred to in all their physical details, and likening them to women who should be conquered and possessed). In a sea the color of blood, the men undertake a physical battle with the dying animals, often sublimated as the ancestral communion of Eros and Thanatos.

The cruelty of the *mattanza* (the characteristic that attracted Salgado to it) is mitigated by the last image of Favignana, a child and his dog at play on the beach, favoring the passage to the next destination, SAN VITO LO CAPO, where the cruel massacre has been reduced to stylized murales. We are treated anew to serenely beautiful panoramas such as that of a seaside town (an important harbor in Roman times) seen from Bonagìa, where a row of benign pedal boats decorate the beach. The image of a farmer riding in the countryside near Bonagìa actually seems like a a projection from another region of Italy, from the Tuscan Maremma, perhaps. While the archaic origins of the island are reconfirmed by the image of the prehistoric graffiti found in the Grotta del Genovese, a cave on LEVANZO facing the waters of the Egadi, to be reached either by boat or on mule-back. These graffiti are important testimony to a remote past: again the theme is of animals (twenty-nine of them in the grotto) and men (four are depicted in the entrance tunnel) – inhabitants of the island of Sicily ten thousand years before our Christian era, immersed in landscapes of undescribable beauty.

The next station is southern Sicily, in the area of the great volcanic cone of ETNA, the Noto valley of Arabic memory. The itinerary touches SIRACUSA, represented by a distracted flower seller and bride, a perfect blend of a portrait with its theatrically white baroque backdrop. After RAGUSA, in IBLA, we are treated to a divertissement, set in the ancient and unique double context of this city split by a valley running between its old and modern parts: an idle cat snoozing atop an antique lion in a pale pink sunlight. The voyage then takes us to NOTO, the emblematic capital of Sicilian baroque, embodied in the contrasting colors of the balloon vendor on the steps of the cathedral of San Niccolò, and by an image of the spectacular *infiorata*, with the city's streets decorated by perfectly ephemeral mosaics of flower petals, of the similar frail beauty as the temporary compositions of street-side *madonnari* chalk-artists.

After a similar dose of condensed culture, the eye longs for the powerful natural stimuli offered by the lakes of VENDÌCARI, an oasis for the flora and fauna of the Siracusa-Pozzallo coastline, a renowned haven for nature-lovers and bird-watchers. While in PACHINO, an important agricultural center founded in 1758 by the principi Giardineli near Portopalo di Capopassero, in a region famous for its red wine and for an especially flavorful variety of tiny cherry tomatoes, we rediscover the value of human labor. The tomato farmers are framed in their greenhouse, offset by the stark geometry of the rows of plants.

In MARZAMENI, a village founded around an old *tonnara* (tuna farm), and home to the noble Villadorata family, Bonavoglia has fixed the image of a piazza reminiscent of the metaphysical cityscapes of DeChirico. It was here that the Taviani brothers chose to shoot some of the most dramatic scenes of their greatest film, *Kaos*. The drama reverberates in the images of the skies above SCICLI, once an Arab stronghold and later a principal town under the Norman reign, and rebuilt to its baroque beauty after the earthquake in 1693. The multiplicity of styles is heightened by the angles the photographer has chosen, making the dominant ruins of the Arabic castle appear distant, and almost unreal. After a stopover at the extraordinary archeological site of Villa del Casale at Piazza Armerina, amid the baroque splendor of MODICA, Bonavoglia draws our attention, ironically, to a single detail of a sensuous nude, chosen from among the wealth of Roman mosaics that have survived – another allusion to the cult of Ceres that we have seen disseminated throughout the whole of Sicily.

uddenly, at 600 meters above sea level, between the Ibla and Erei mountains, we arrive in CALTAGIRONE. The pottery vases made here were famous throughout antiquity – indeed, some interpret the original Arabic name Cal'at Ghiran to mean "the Castle of Vases." And to this day, the town, also known as the "Sicilian Faenza," is enlivened by a wealth of traditional ceramics. The spectacular stairway leading up to the church of Santa Maria del Monte, each of its 142 steps decorated with majolica motifs dating from the tenth to the twentieth centuries, stands as an emblem of the city. Ever since 1606, these extraordinary steps unite the lower city with San Giuliano, the upper part of town.

Already the meanderings through the "great book" of Sicily are drawing to a close. The last legs of the trip are in the northeastern regions, under the dominating profile of ETNA, Europe's largest volcano, which is still actively fuming. Locally, the volcano represents a kind of deity, all-powerful over human destinies; it is referred to namelessly, simply as *iddu*, or "him." More than once the Ionic coastline has succumbed to its fiery eruptions – in 1669, the devastating magma reached as far as Catania and the sea. But while the lava has rendered the landscape surrounding the pointed cone (known also as Mongibello, "the mountain of mountains," from the Italian "monte" and the Arabic "gebel," again meaning "mountain") curiously lunar, at the same time it has made the soil fertile, and a lush destination for all sorts of voyagers, from the Greek colonizers, who landed in 734 B.C. and founded the city of Naxos, up to the Grand Tour travelers of the eighteenth century. It is perhaps the most famous part of the island, crowded with visitors in the summer months, when the orange blossoms perfume the air and the gardens are in full flower, but well frequented also in winter, when the snow caps Etna's summit. Bonavoglia peruses the area with his particular gaze, and in ACITREZZA, a fishing village where Giovanni Verga set *I Malavoglia* and Visconti filmed *La Terra Trema*, he captures the dive of a youngster from atop one of the *faraglione* known as the "Ciclopi," in reference to the stones that Polyphemus hurled into the sea in his blind rage against Ulysses. The village has been declared part of a "literary park," while the waters are now a natural marine reserve.

In ACIREALE, the largest of the seven cities east of the volcano, the facades of churches and cathedrals are particular examples of baroque magnificence. The legend surrounding the city's name relates to the story of love between a shepherd by the name of Acis and his beloved water-nymph, Galatea. Polyphemus, so the legend has it, vented his jealousy on Acis by crushing him with a boulder. In merciful intervention, the gods turned the shepherd into a river running underground, allowing him to join his beloved in the sea. And it is on a similarly mythological note that we arrive at the last station of this Sicilian peregrination, amid the seven sisters of the EOLIAN ARCHIPELAGO. From Stromboli to Vulcano and Lipari, a symphony of sunlight and natural panoramas leads us from the harvest of Malvasia grapes on Salina up to the very last image of the book, a sort of emblematic provocation: a female figure, vulcanic lava–black, lies lazily reclined at the edge of a turquoise swimming pool. She is a siren to the white-haired swimmer who is nearing her. This Eolian temptress, the last piece of this mosaic portrait of the island, is the embodiment of Sicilia herself. The extraordinary cultural and natural palimpsest that is Sicily, however partially or subjectively perceived, cannot but occasion a universal desire to discover, or rediscover, the breathtaking beauty to be experienced here. In a land whose fate lies in an ancient, ineluctable ambivalence: those who stay here, always dream of leaving; those who leave, dream only of returning.

Donatella Trotta

SICILY ~

ABOVE A shepherd and his flock in the summery hills of Enna

ABOVE RIGHT Springtime in the lonely hills of Cammarata

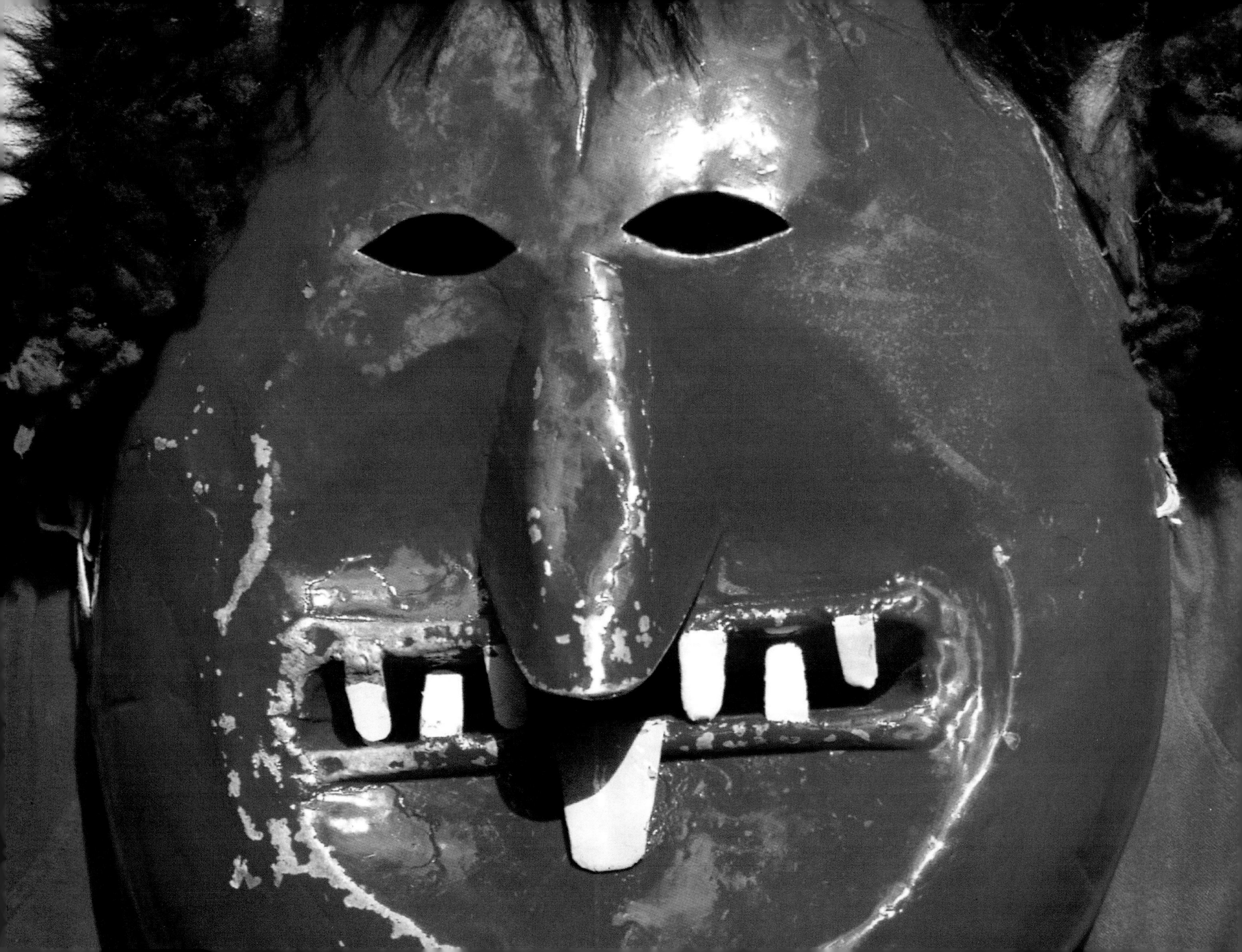

LEFT The "Ballu de li Diavuli" held in Prizzi at Easter is an ancient pre-Christian ritual symbolizing the battle between Good and Evil

ABOVE The whole town of Prizzi is covered in artistic mural paintings

BELOW The "red devil" and the yellow representatives of Death chase each other in the "Ballu de li diavuli" held in Prizzi

BELOW RIGHT Two old women watch the procession from their home

RIGHT In a syncretism of Christianity and paganism, the image of the madonna is called upon to oversee the "Ballu de li diavuli" Easter rites

FAR RIGHT One of the "diavuli" during his dance amidst the Prizzi crowd

RIGHT Horses in the Madonie National Park

LEFT The medieval village of Sperlinga in the Madonìe hills

BELOW The town of Gangi covers its hill like the ring on cake

RIGHT The ancient art of falconeering introduced in Sicily in the 13th century by Frederick II is still practiced in Geraci Siculo

FAR RIGHT A falconeer and his falcon

FAR LEFT A rider and his horse in Petralia Sottana

LEFT The wedding march preluding the "Cordella dance" in Petralia Sottana

RIGHT A girl participating in a wedding march

CENTER The musicians await the bride in the piazza in front of her house

FAR RIGHT
The "Cordella dance"

LEFT The ceramics produced in S. Stefano di Camastra are renowned

ABOVE A young girl at work decorating traditional ceramics

RIGHT The exquisite romantic architecture of the cathedral at Cefalu' stands as a testimony to the city's history as the center of the reaffirmation of Christianity in Sicily after the expulsion of the Moors

FAR RIGHT The lakes at Tindari

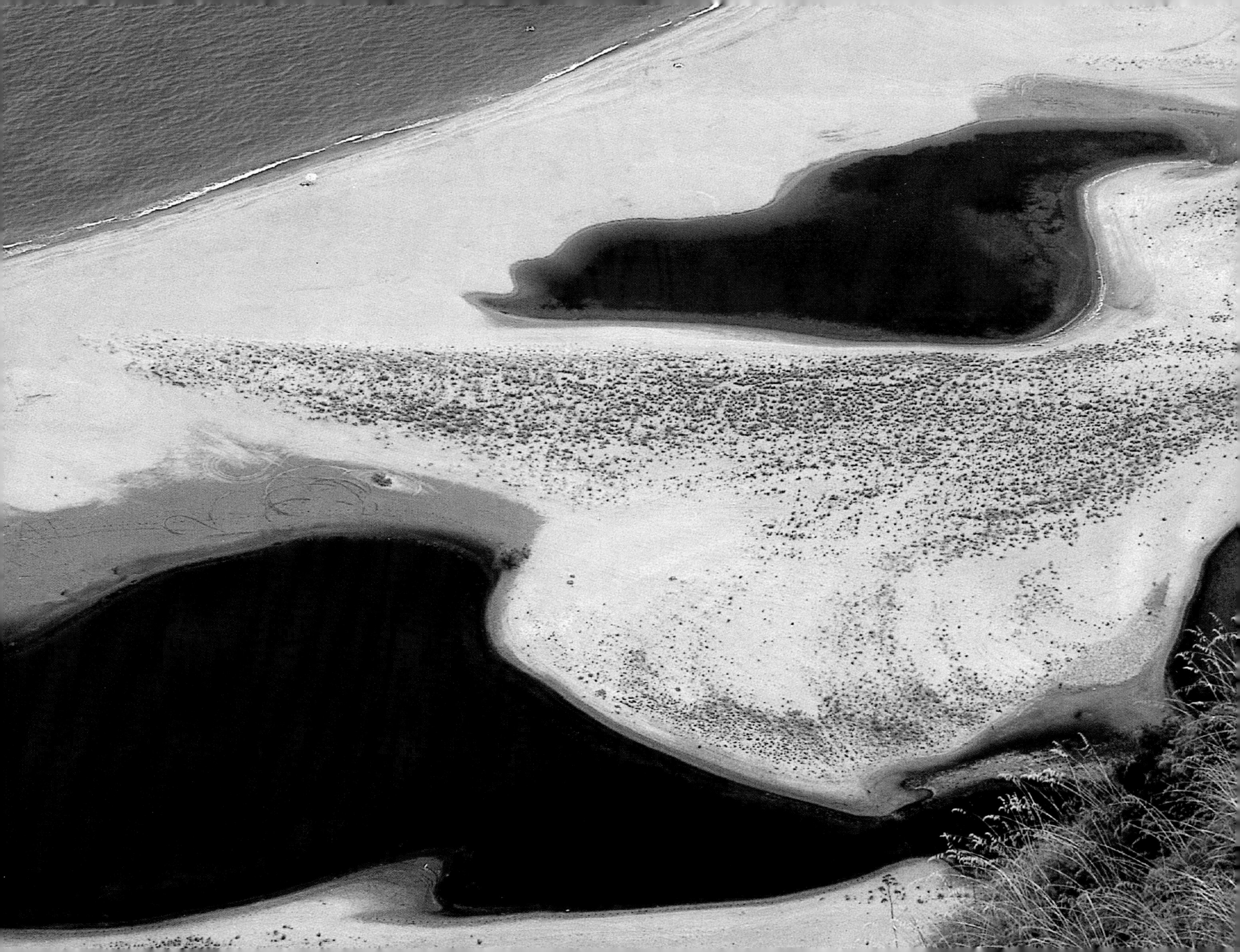

FAR LEFT The St. Joseph "cunnuta" festival in Mezzojuso

LEFT Traditional ornaments adorning a mule's tail during the festivity of St. Joseph in Mezzojuso

ABOVE A pastel colored country side house in Ciminna hills

RIGHT A Sicilian cowboy

OPERA DEI PUPI

PREVIOUS PAGE, TOP LEFT
A girl carrying votive offerings during a procession in honor of the child martyr San Vito in Ciminna

PREVIOUS PAGE, BOTTOM LEFT The child behind bars represents the young San Vito in prison

PREVIOUS PAGE, CENTER
Monreale, Mural of traditional sicilian puppet show

PREVIOUS PAGE, TOP RIGHT
Monreale, Ceramic shop

PREVIOUS PAGE, BOTTOM RIGHT A detail of a colorful Sicilian traditional cart

LEFT Mummifying their beloved was a practice of the 19th century clerical and bourgeois class in Palermo

ABOVE LEFT Palermo, La Martorana is a reminder of the Arab civilization in Sicily

ABOVE The Cathedral

23

FAR LEFT Palermo, children in Piazza Marina

LEFT A tunafish monger in the Ballaro' market

LEFT Palermo, Groom await his bride in a church in the popular section of Ballaro'

RIGHT Palermo, the float carrying the statue of S. Rosalia during her annual festival is changed every year

FAR RIGHT Sacred and profane are mixed in the St. Rosalia festival

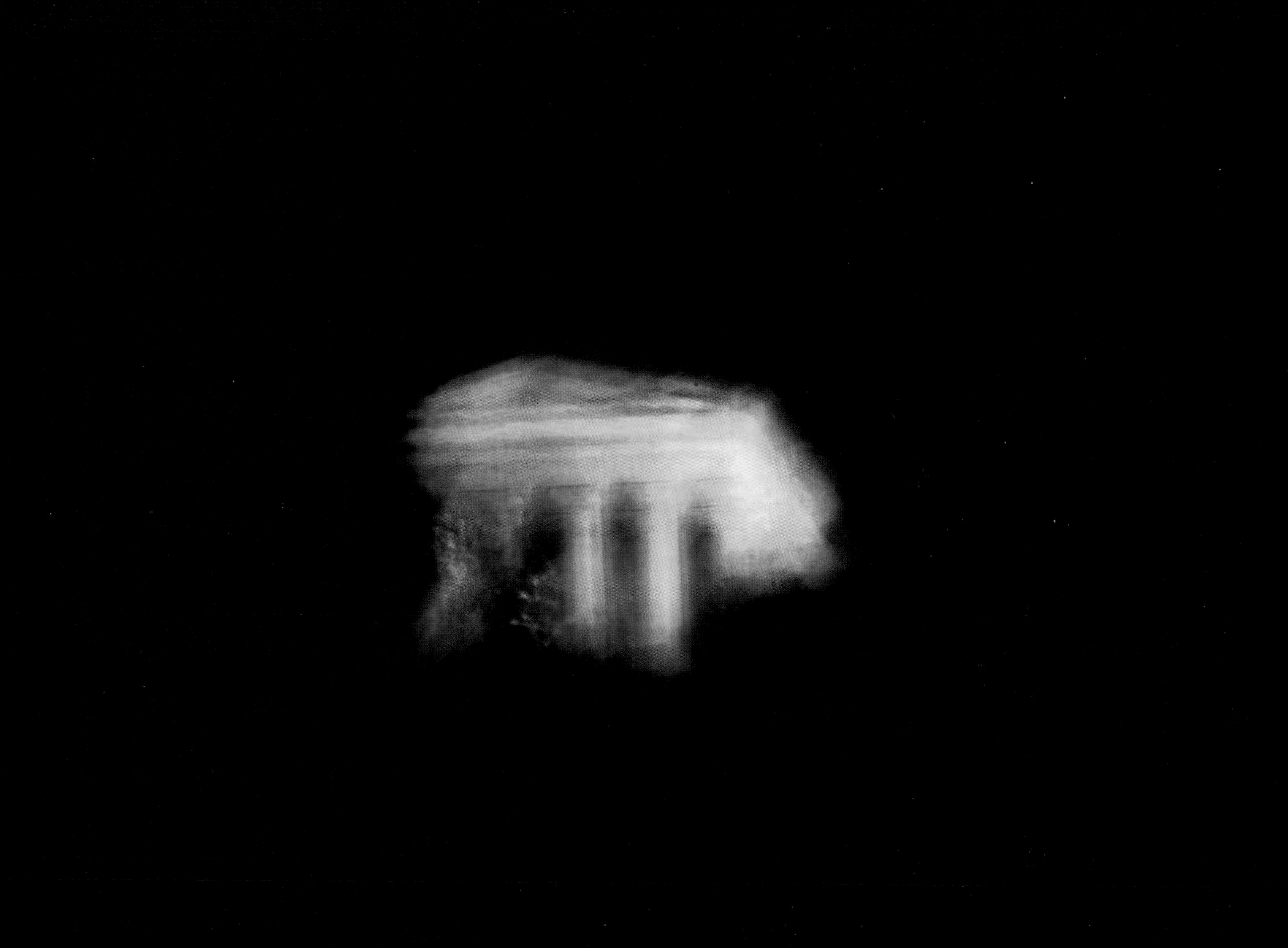

PREVIOUS PAGE A ghost-like image of the temple at Segesta

LEFT The Segesta country side

RIGHT, CENTER Erice, youngsters in traditional costume participate in one of the frequent historical reenactments

FAR RIGHT The Cathedral of Erice dates back to the 14th century

ABOVE Mazara del Vallo, on the facade of the cathedral, a Christian knight dominates a defeated Moor

ABOVE RIGHT The port and "casbah" of Mazara are home to a sizable community of immigrants from nearby Tunisia

LEFT Mozia (Marsala) The curiously Northern European windmills are an unexpected counterpoint in the Mediterranean landscape of the salt lakes

ABOVE A windmill at the salt-lakes of Mozia

LEFT The mounds of salt are protected with clay roof-tiles

BELOW LEFT Trapani, onlookers during the procession of the "Misteri" which takes place in the Holy Week

BELOW The presence of girls offering wheat during the procession derives from the ancient cult of Ceres, the goddess of fertility

ABOVE A woman participating in the procession of the "Misteri"

ABOVE CENTER One of the 22 "Misteri" sculptural groups made of papier maché and wood representing the stations of the Via Crucis

ABOVE RIGHT The organizers of the procession embrace at the end of the 22 hours festivity of the "Misteri" in Trapani

ABOVE The procession of the "Misteri" in Trapani

RIGHT During the "Misteri" procession

BELOW Fishing nets in the wonderful sea of Bonagia Islands

BELOW RIGHT Time-worn tuna boats in Bonagìa

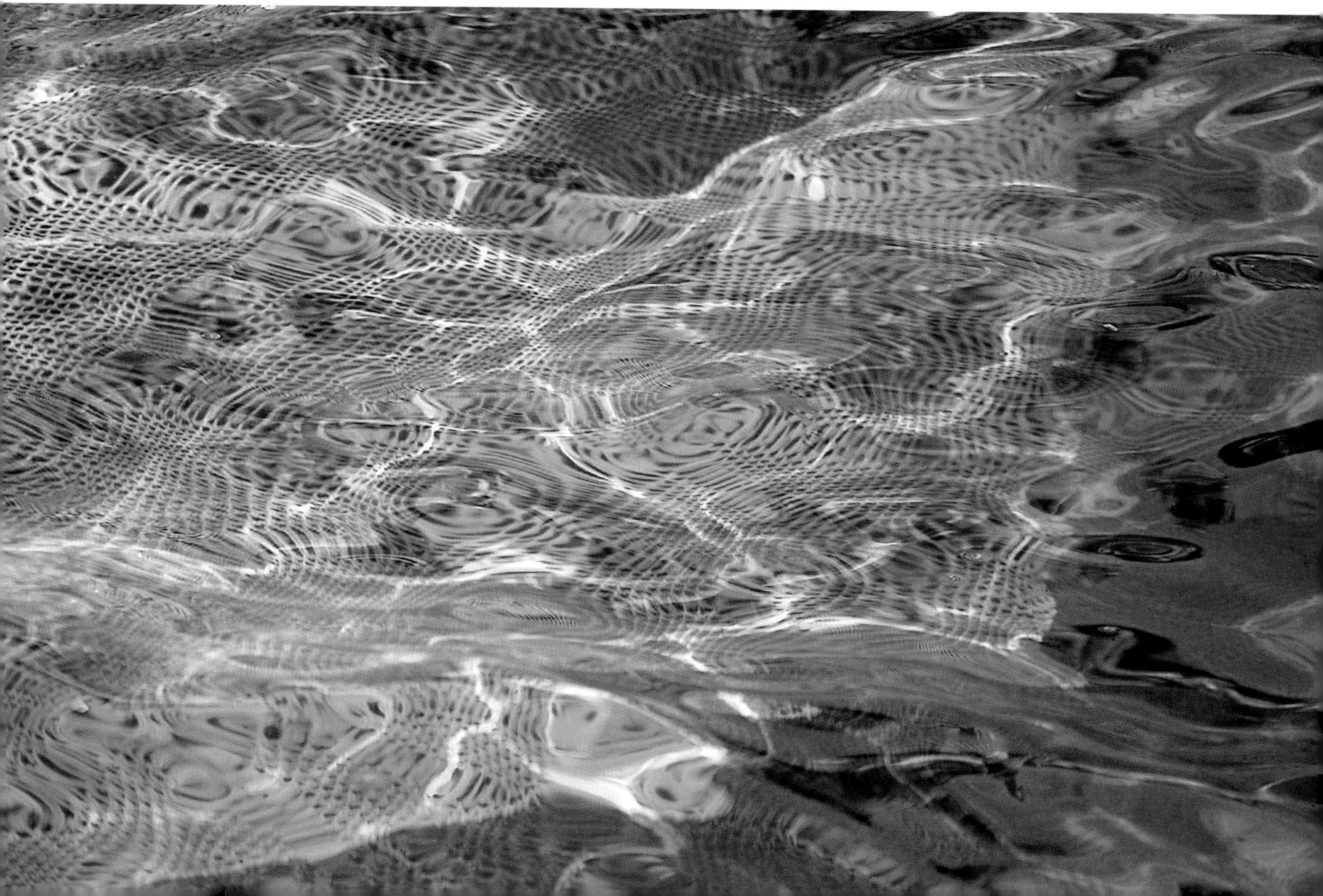

LEFT The old *tonnara* of Trapani now is considered an archeological site

ABOVE Boy and his dog on the Favignana beach (Egadi Islands)

ABOVE LEFT Boats heading to the *mattanza* field

ABOVE The *rais* of the *mattanza* on the lookout for the tunafish

ABOVE The one-to-one battle of the *mattanza*

ABOVE RIGHT The *mattanza* is the event of the year in Favignana

RIGHT The romantic bay of Levanzo (Egadi Islands)

FAR RIGHT Two seagulls and a boat in the tiny Levanzo harbor

ABOVE LEFT A moment of "macho" rest for these tunafish catchers

ABOVE CENTER Levanzo, the prehistoric graffiti in the "Grotta del Genovese" are 10,000 years old

ABOVE The beach of S. Vito Lo Capo is a paradise for sunbathers

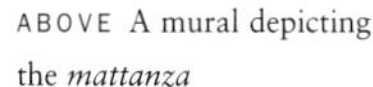

ABOVE A mural depicting the *mattanza*

RIGHT A typical Sicilian horseman in S. Vito Lo Capo countryside

RIGHT Old fishing boats on Bonagia shore

LEFT The cathedral of Noto

RIGHT, FAR RIGHT The celebrated *infiorata* of Noto

Antichità

FAR LEFT A flower girl in the Siracusa market

LEFT A bride prepares entering the Cathedral in Siracusa

RIGHT Marzameni is a lovely fisherman village south of Siracusa

FAR RIGHT The wildlife reserve of Vindicari

RIGHT Farmers of Pachino harvesting the sweetest tomatoes in the world

S MATTIA
Duomo di
S. Pietro
1959
MARIA SS. SCAL
DEL PARADISO

LEFT Modica, Chiesa di San Pietro

FAR LEFT Modica, Duomo di San Giorgio

CENTER Scicli, the Arab castle dominates the baroque style town

LEFT A cat resting at the sunset in Ragusa/Ibla

ABOVE Mosaics in the Roman villa at Piazza Armerina

ABOVE RIGHT Caltagirone, the stairway of the Annunziata is covered with ceramic tiles

RIGHT Boys diving off the "Ciclopi" crags in Acitrezza bay

FAR LEFT The church of S. Bartolomeo in Acireale

LEFT Acireale, the Cathedral

PREVIOUS PAGE A tranquil moment on the Etna vulcano

ABOVE Tourist buses in the lunar landscape of the Etna

ABOVE RIGHT Etna park rangers making gift items from fresh lava

Shell
SUPER GREASE

RIGHT The isle of Vulcano, as seen from Lipari

LEFT Eolian style house in Salina (Eolian Islands)

BELOW The malvasia harvest in Salina, home of the renowned dessert wine

BELOW RIGHT Strombolicchio, Stromboli's island "little brother"

RIGHT Tourists bathing in the thermal mud on Vulcano Island

FAR LEFT A view of Stromboli Island from Salina Island lighthouse

LEFT A poolside siren sculpted in lava at the Hotel "La Sciara" in Stromboli

IMAGES

WESTERN SICILY

22. Enna
23. Cammarata
24. Prizzi
30. Madonie National Park
Sperlinga
Gangi
Geraci Siculo
Petralia Sottana
40. S. Stefano di Camastra
42. Cefalu'
43. Tindari
44. Mezzojuso
46. Ciminna
48. Monreale
50. Palermo
60. Segesta
64. Erice
66. Mazara del Vallo
68. Mozia (Marsala)
72. Trapani
78. Bonagia (Trapani)
81. Egadi
89. San Vito lo Capo

SOUTHERN SICILY

Baroque Cities
94. *Noto*
98. *Siracusa*
104. *Modica*
106. *Scicli*
107. *Ragusa/Ibla*
109. *Caltagirone*

EAST SICILY

110. Acitrezza
112. Acireale
114. Etna
118. Eolie